The Democracy
of Species

The Democracy of Species

ROBIN WALL KIMMERER

PENGUIN BOOKS — GREEN IDEAS

PENGUIN BOOKS

UK | USA | Canada | Ireland | Australia
India | New Zealand | South Africa

Penguin Books is part of the Penguin Random House group of companies
whose addresses can be found at global.penguinrandomhouse.com.

First published in *Braiding Sweetgrass: Indigenous Wisdom,
Scientific Knowledge, and the Teachings of Plants* by Milkweed Editions 2013
This extract published in Penguin Books 2021

005

Copyright © Robin Wall Kimmerer, 2013

The moral right of the author has been asserted

Set in 12.2/15pt Dante MT Std
Typeset by Jouve (UK), Milton Keynes
Printed and bound in Great Britain by Clays Ltd, Elcograf S.p.A.

The authorized representative in the EEA is Penguin Random House Ireland,
Morrison Chambers, 32 Nassau Street, Dublin D02 YH68

A CIP catalogue record for this book is available from the British Library

ISBN: 978-0-141-99704-9

www.greenpenguin.co.uk

Contents

Learning the Grammar of Animacy

*To be native to a place we must learn
to speak its language.*

I come here to listen, to nestle in the curve of
the roots in a soft hollow of pine needles, to lean
my bones against the column of white pine, to
turn off the voice in my head until I can hear
the voices outside it: the *shhh* of wind in needles,
water trickling over rock, nuthatch tapping, chip-
munks digging, beechnut falling, mosquito in my
ear, and something more – something that is not
me, for which we have no language, the wordless
being of others in which we are never alone. After
the drumbeat of my mother's heart, *this* was my
first language.

I could spend a whole day listening. And a whole
night. And in the morning, without my hearing

it, there might be a mushroom that was not there the night before, creamy white, pushed up from the pine needle duff, out of darkness to light, still glistening with the fluid of its passage. *Puhpowee.*

Listening in wild places, we are audience to conversations in a language not our own. I think now that it was a longing to comprehend this language I hear in the woods that led me to science, to learn over the years to speak fluent botany. A tongue that should not, by the way, be mistaken for the language of plants. I did learn another language in science, though, one of careful observation, an intimate vocabulary that names each little part. To name and describe you must first see, and science polishes the gift of seeing. I honor the strength of the language that has become a second tongue to me. But beneath the richness of its vocabulary and its descriptive power, something is missing, the same something that swells around you and in you when you listen to the world. Science can be a language of distance which reduces a being to its working parts; it is a language of objects. The language scientists speak, however precise, is based on a profound error in grammar, an omission, a grave loss in translation from the native languages of these shores.

My first taste of the missing language was the word *Puhpowee* on my tongue. I stumbled upon it in a book by the Anishinaabe ethno-botanist Keewaydinoquay, in a treatise on the traditional uses of fungi by our people. *Puhpowee*, she explained, translates as 'the force which causes mushrooms to push up from the earth overnight.' As a biologist, I was stunned that such a word existed. In all its technical vocabulary, Western science has no such term, no words to hold this mystery. You'd think that biologists, of all people, would have words for life. But in scientific language our terminology is used to define the boundaries of our knowing. What lies beyond our grasp remains unnamed.

In the three syllables of this new word I could see an entire process of close observation in the damp morning woods, the formulation of a theory for which English has no equivalent. The makers of this word understood a world of being, full of unseen energies that animate everything.

I've cherished it for many years, as a talisman, and longed for the people who gave a name to the life force of mushrooms. The language that holds *Puhpowee* is one that I wanted to speak. So when I learned that the word for rising, for emergence, belonged to the language of my ancestors, it became a signpost for me.

Had history been different, I would likely speak Bodewadmimwin, or Potawatomi, an Anishinaabe language. But, like many of the three hundred and fifty indigenous languages of the Americas, Potawatomi is threatened, and I speak the language you read. The powers of assimilation did their work as my chance of hearing that language, and yours too, was washed from the mouths of Indian children in government boarding schools where speaking your native tongue was forbidden. Children like my grandfather, who was taken from his family when he was just a little boy of nine years old. This history scattered not only our words but also our people. Today I live far from our reservation, so even if I could speak the language, I would have no one to talk to. But a few summers ago, at our yearly tribal gathering, a language class was held and I slipped into the tent to listen.

There was a great deal of excitement about the class because, for the first time, every single fluent speaker in our tribe would be there as a teacher. When the speakers were called forward to the circle of folding chairs, they moved slowly – with canes, walkers, and wheelchairs, only a few entirely under their own power. I counted them as they filled the chairs. Nine. Nine fluent speakers. In the whole world. Our language, millennia in the making, sits in those nine chairs. The words that praised creation, told the old stories, lulled my ancestors to sleep, rests today in the tongues of nine very mortal men and women. Each in turn addresses the small group of would-be students.

A man with long gray braids tells how his mother hid him away when the Indian agents came to take the children. He escaped boarding school by hiding under an overhung bank where the sound of the stream covered his crying. The others were all taken and had their mouths washed out with soap, or worse, for 'talking that dirty Indian language.' Because he alone stayed home and was raised up calling the plants and animals by the name the Creator gave them, he is here today, a carrier of the language. The engines of assimilation worked well. The speaker's eyes blaze as he tells us, 'We're the end of the road. We are all that is left. If you young people do not learn, the language will die. The missionaries and the U.S. government will have their victory at last.'

A great-grandmother from the circle pushes her walker up close to the microphone. 'It's not just the words that will be lost,' she says. 'The language is the heart of our culture; it holds our thoughts, our way of seeing the world. It's too beautiful for English to explain.' *Puhpowee.*

Jim Thunder, at seventy-five the youngest of the speakers, is a round brown man of serious demeanor who spoke only in Potawatomi. He began solemnly, but as he warmed to his subject his voice lifted like a breeze in the birch trees and his hands began to tell the story. He became more and more animated, rising to his feet, holding us

rapt and silent although almost no one understood a single word. He paused as if reaching the
climax of his story and looked out at the audience with a twinkle of expectation. One of the
grandmothers behind him covered her mouth in
a giggle and his stern face suddenly broke into a
smile as big and sweet as a cracked watermelon.
He bent over laughing and the grandmas dabbed
away tears of laughter, holding their sides, while
the rest of us looked on in wonderment. When
the laughter subsided, he spoke at last in English:
'What will happen to a joke when no one can
hear it anymore? How lonely those words will
be, when their power is gone. Where will they
go? Off to join the stories that can never be told
again.'

So now my house is spangled with Post-it notes
in another language, as if I were studying for a
trip abroad. But I'm not going away, I'm coming
home.

Ni pi je ezhyayen? asks the little yellow sticky note
on my back door. My hands are full and the car
is running, but I switch my bag to the other hip

7

and pause long enough to respond. *Odanek nde zhya*, I'm going to town. And so I do, to work, to class, to meetings, to the bank, to the grocery store. I talk all day and sometimes write all evening in the beautiful language I was born to, the same one used by 70 percent of the world's people, a tongue viewed as the most useful, with the richest vocabulary in the modern world. English. When I get home at night to my quiet house, there is a faithful Post-it note on the closet door. *Gisken I gbiskewagen!* And so I take off my coat.

I cook dinner, pulling utensils from cupboards labeled *emkwanen, nagen*. I have become a woman who speaks Potawatomi to household objects. When the phone rings I barely glance at the Post-it there as I *dopnen* the *giktogan*. And whether it is a solicitor or a friend, they speak English. Once a week or so, it is my sister from the West Coast who says *Bozho. Mokthewenkwe nda* – as if she needed to identify herself: who else speaks Potawatomi? To call it speaking is a stretch. Really, all we do is blurt garbled phrases to each other in a parody of conversation: How are you? I am fine. Go to town. See bird. Red. Frybread good. We sound like Tonto's side of the Hollywood dialogue with the Lone Ranger. 'Me try talk good Injun way.' On the rare occasion when we actually can string together a halfway coherent thought, we freely insert high school Spanish words to fill in the gaps, making a language we call Spanawatomi.

Tuesdays and Thursdays at 12:15 Oklahoma time, I join the Potawatomi lunchtime language class, streaming from tribal headquarters via the Internet. There are usually about ten of us, from all over the country. Together we learn to count and to say *pass the salt*. Someone asks, 'How do you say *please* pass the salt?' Our teacher, Justin Neely, a young man devoted to language revival, explains that while there are several words for *thank you*, there is no word for *please*. Food was meant to be shared, no added politeness needed; it was simply a cultural given that one was asking respectfully. The missionaries took this absence as further evidence of crude manners.

Many nights, when I should be grading papers or paying bills, I'm at the computer running through Potawatomi language drills. After months, I have mastered the kindergarten vocabulary and can confidently match the pictures of animals to their indigenous names. It reminds me of reading picture books to my children: 'Can you point to the squirrel? Where is the bunny?' All the while I'm telling myself that I really don't have time for this, and what's more, little need to know the words for *bass* and *fox* anyway. Since our tribal diaspora left us scattered to the four winds, who would I talk to?

The simple phrases I'm learning are perfect for my dog. Sit! Eat! Come here! Be quiet! But since she scarcely responds to these commands in English, I'm reluctant to train her to be bilingual. An admiring student once asked me if I spoke my native language. I was tempted to say, 'Oh yes, we speak Potawatomi at home' – me, the dog, and the Post-it notes. Our teacher tells us not to be discouraged and thanks us every time a word is spoken – thanks us for breathing life into the language, even if we only speak a single word. 'But I have no one to talk to,' I complain. 'None of us do,' he reassures me, 'but someday we will.'

So I dutifully learn the vocabulary but find it hard to see the 'heart of our culture' in translating *bed* and *sink* into Potawatomi. Learning nouns was pretty easy; after all, I'd learned thousands of botanical Latin names and scientific terms. I reasoned that this could not be too much different – just a one-for-one substitution, memorization. At least on paper, where you can see the letters, this is true. Hearing the language is a different story. There are fewer letters in our alphabet, so the distinction among words for a beginner is often subtle. With the beautiful clusters of consonants of *zh* and *mb* and *shwe* and *kwe* and *mshk*, our language sounds like wind in the pines and water over rocks, sounds our ears may have been more delicately attuned to in the past, but no longer. To learn again, you really have to listen.

To actually *speak*, of course, requires verbs, and here is where my kindergarten proficiency at naming things leaves off. English is a noun-based language, somehow appropriate to a culture so obsessed with things. Only 30 percent of English words are verbs, but in Potawatomi that proportion is 70 percent. Which means that 70 percent of the words have to be conjugated, and 70 percent have different tenses and cases to be mastered.

European languages often assign gender to nouns, but Potawatomi does not divide the world into masculine and feminine. Nouns and verbs both are animate and inanimate. You hear a person with a word that is completely different from the one with which you hear an airplane. Pronouns, articles, plurals, demonstratives, verbs – all those syntactical bits I never could keep straight in high school English are all aligned in Potawatomi to provide different ways to speak of the living world and the lifeless one. Different verb forms, different plurals, different everything apply depending on whether what you are speaking of is alive.

No wonder there are only nine speakers left! I try, but the complexity makes my head hurt and my ear can barely distinguish between words that mean completely different things. One teacher reassures us that this will come with practice, but another elder concedes that these close similarities are inherent in the language. As Stewart King, a knowledge keeper and great teacher, reminds us, the Creator meant for us to laugh, so humor is deliberately built into the syntax. Even a small slip of the tongue can convert 'We need more firewood' to 'Take off your clothes.' In fact, I learned that the mystical word *Puhpowee* is used not only for mushrooms, but also for certain other shafts that rise mysteriously in the night.

My sister's gift to me one Christmas was a set of magnetic tiles for the refrigerator in Ojibwe, or Anishinabemowin, a language closely related to Potawatomi. I spread them out on my kitchen table looking for familiar words, but the more I looked, the more worried I got. Among the hundred or more tiles, there was but a single word that I recognized: *megwech,* thank you. The small feeling of accomplishment from months of study evaporated in a moment.

I remember paging through the Ojibwe dictionary she sent, trying to decipher the tiles, but the spellings didn't always match and the print was too small and there are way too many variations on a single word and I was feeling that this was just way too hard. The threads in my brain knotted and the harder I tried, the tighter they became. Pages blurred and my eyes settled on a word – a verb, of course: 'to be a Saturday.' *Pfft!* I threw down the book. Since when is *Saturday* a verb? Everyone knows it's a noun. I grabbed the dictionary and flipped more pages and all kinds of things seemed to be verbs: 'to be a hill,' 'to be red,' 'to be a long sandy stretch of beach,' and then my finger rested on *wiikwegamaa*: 'to be a bay.' 'Ridiculous!' I ranted in my head. 'There is no reason to make it so complicated. No wonder no one speaks it. A cumbersome language, impossible to learn, and more than that, it's all wrong. A bay is most definitely a person, place, or thing – a noun and not a verb.' I was ready to give up. I'd learned a few words, done my duty to the language that was taken from my grandfather. Oh, the ghosts of the missionaries in the boarding schools must have been rubbing their hands in glee at my frustration. 'She's going to surrender,' they said.

And then I swear I heard the zap of synapses

firing. An electric current sizzled down my arm and through my finger, and practically scorched the page where that one word lay. In that moment I could smell the water of the bay, watch it rock against the shore and hear it sift onto the sand. A bay is a noun only if water is *dead*. When *bay* is a noun, it is defined by humans, trapped between its shores and contained by the word. But the verb *wiikwegamaa* – to *be* a bay – releases the water from bondage and lets it live. 'To be a bay' holds the wonder that, for this moment, the living water has decided to shelter itself between these shores, conversing with cedar roots and a flock of baby mergansers. Because it could do otherwise – become a stream or an ocean or a waterfall, and there are verbs for that, too. To be a hill, to be a sandy beach, to be a Saturday, all are possible verbs in a world where everything is alive. Water, land, and even a day, the language a mirror for seeing the animacy of the world, the life that pulses through all things, through pines and nuthatches and mushrooms. *This* is the language I hear in the woods; this is the language that lets us speak of what wells up all around us.

And the vestiges of boarding schools, the soap-wielding missionary wraiths, hang their heads in defeat.

This is the grammar of animacy. Imagine seeing your grandmother standing at the stove in her apron and then saying of her, 'Look, it is making soup. It has gray hair.' We might snicker at such a mistake, but we also recoil from it. In English, we never refer to a member of our family, or indeed to any person, as *it*. That would be a profound act of disrespect. *It* robs a person of selfhood and kinship, reducing a person to a mere thing. So it is that in Potawatomi and most other indigenous languages, we use the same words to address the living world as we use for our family. Because they are our family.

To whom does our language extend the grammar of animacy? Naturally, plants and animals are animate, but as I learn, I am discovering that the Potawatomi understanding of what it means to be animate diverges from the list of attributes of living beings we all learned in Biology 101. In Potawatomi 101, rocks are animate, as are mountains and water and fire and places. Beings that are imbued with spirit, our sacred medicines, our songs, drums, and even stories, are all animate. The list of the inanimate seems to be smaller, filled with objects that are made by people. Of an inanimate being, like a table, we say, '*What* is it?' And we answer *Dopwen yewe.* Table it is. But of apple, we must say, '*Who* is that being?' And reply *Mshimin yawe.* Apple that being is.

Yawe – the animate *to be.* I am, you are, s/he is. To speak of those possessed with life and spirit we must say *yawe.* By what linguistic confluence do Yahweh of the Old Testament and *yawe* of the New World both fall from the mouths of the reverent? Isn't this just what it means, to be, to have the breath of life within, to be the offspring of Creation? The language reminds us, in every sentence, of our kinship with all of the animate world.

English doesn't give us many tools for incorporating respect for animacy. In English, you are either a human or a thing. Our grammar boxes us in by the choice of reducing a nonhuman being to an *it,* or it must be gendered, inappropriately, as a *he* or a *she.* Where are our words for the simple existence of another living being? Where is our *yawe?* My friend Michael Nelson, an ethicist who thinks a great deal about moral inclusion, told me about a woman he knows, a field biologist whose work is among other-than-humans. Most of her companions are not two-legged, and so her language has shifted to accommodate her relationships. She kneels along the trail to inspect a set of moose tracks, saying, 'Someone's already been this way this morning.' 'Someone is in my hat,' she says, shaking out a deerfly. Someone, not something.

When I am in the woods with my students, teaching them the gifts of plants and how to call them by name, I try to be mindful of my language, to be bilingual between the lexicon of science and the grammar of animacy. Although they still have to learn scientific roles and Latin names, I hope I am also teaching them to know the world as a neighborhood of nonhuman residents, to know that, as ecotheologian Thomas Berry has written, 'we must say of the universe that it is a communion of subjects, not a collection of objects.'

One afternoon, I sat with my field ecology students by a *wiikwegamaa* and shared this idea of animate language. One young man, Andy, splashing his feet in the clear water, asked the big question. 'Wait a second,' he said as he wrapped his mind around this linguistic distinction, 'doesn't this mean that speaking English, thinking in English, somehow gives us permission to disrespect nature? By denying everyone else the right to be persons? Wouldn't things be different if nothing was an *it*?'

Swept away with the idea, he said it felt like an awakening to him. More like a remembering, I think. The animacy of the world is something we already know, but the language of animacy teeters on extinction – not just for Native peoples, but for everyone. Our toddlers speak of plants and animals as if they were people, extending to them self and intention and compassion – until we teach them not to. We quickly retrain them and make them forget. When we tell them that the tree is not a *who*, but an *it*, we make that maple an object; we put a barrier between us, absolving ourselves of moral responsibility and opening the door to exploitation. Saying *it* makes a living land into 'natural resources.' If a maple is an *it*, we can take up the chain saw. If a maple is a *her*, we think twice.

Another student countered Andy's argument. 'But we can't say *he* or *she*. That would be anthropomorphism.' They are well-schooled biologists who have been instructed, in no uncertain terms, never to ascribe human characteristics to a study object, to another species. It's a cardinal sin that leads to a loss of objectivity. Carla pointed out that 'it's also disrespectful to the animals. We shouldn't project our perceptions onto them. They have their own ways – they're not just people in furry costumes.' Andy countered, 'But just because we don't think of them as humans doesn't mean they aren't beings. Isn't it even more disrespectful to assume that we're the only species that counts as "persons"?' The arrogance of English is that the only way to be animate, to be worthy of respect and moral concern, is to be a human.

A language teacher I know explained that grammar is just the way we chart relationships in language. Maybe it also reflects our relationships with each other. Maybe a grammar of animacy could lead us to whole new ways of living in the world, other species a sovereign people, a world with a democracy of species, not a tyranny of one – with moral responsibility to water and wolves, and with a legal system that recognizes the standing of other species. It's all in the pronouns.

Andy is right. Learning the grammar of animacy could well be a restraint on our mindless exploitation of land. But there is more to it. I have heard our elders give advice like 'You should go among the standing people' or 'Go spend some time with those Beaver people.' They remind us of the capacity of others as our teachers, as holders of knowledge, as guides. Imagine walking through a richly inhabited world of Birch people, Bear people, Rock people, beings we think of and therefore speak of as persons worthy of our respect, of inclusion in a peopled world. We Americans are reluctant to learn a foreign language of our own species, let alone another species. But imagine the possibilities. Imagine the access we would have to different perspectives, the things we might see through other eyes, the wisdom that surrounds us. We don't have to figure out everything by ourselves: there are intelligences other than our own, teachers all around us. Imagine how much less lonely the world would be.

Every word I learn comes with a breath of gratitude for our elders who have kept this language alive and passed along its poetry. I still struggle mightily with verbs, can hardly speak at all, and I'm still most adept with only kindergarten vocabulary. But I like that in the morning I can go for my walk around the meadow greeting neighbors by name. When Crow caws at me from the hedgerow, I can call back *Mno gizhget andush-ukwe!* I can brush my hand over the soft grasses and murmur *Bozho mishkos.* It's a small thing, but it makes me happy.

I'm not advocating that we all learn Potawatomi or Hopi or Seminole, even if we could. Immigrants came to these shores bearing a legacy of languages, all to be cherished. But to become native to this place, if we are to survive here, and our neighbors too, our work is to learn to speak the grammar of animacy, so that we might truly be at home.

I remember the words of Bill Tall Bull, a Cheyenne elder. As a young person, I spoke to him with a heavy heart, lamenting that I had no native language with which to speak to the plants and the places that I love. 'They love to hear the old language,' he said, 'it's true.' 'But,' he said, with fingers on his lips, 'You don't have to speak it here.' 'If you speak it here,' he said, patting his chest, 'They will hear you.'

The Honorable Harvest

The crows see me coming across the field, a woman with a basket, and argue my provenance loudly among themselves. The soil is hard under my feet, bare except for a scattering of plow-scraped rocks and a few of last year's corn stalks, their remnant prop roots squatting like bleached-out spider legs. Years of herbicides and continuous corn have left the field sterile. Even in rain-soaked April not a blade of green shows its face. By August it will once again be a monoculture of corn plants in straight rows of indentured servitude, but for now it's my cross-country route to the woods.

My entourage of crows leaves me at the stone wall, a loose windrow of glacial cobbles raked from the field to mark its boundary. On the other

side the ground is soft underfoot and deep in cen-
turies of leaf mold, the forest floor flocked with
tiny pink spring beauties and clumps of yellow
violets. The humus stirs with trout lilies and trillium poised to rise through the winter-brown mat
of leaves. A wood thrush hangs a silvery trill on
the still-bare branches of the maples. The dense
patches of leeks are among the first to appear in
the spring, their green so vivid that they signal
like a neon sign: PICK ME!

I resist the urge to answer their call immedi-
ately and instead address the plants the way I've
been taught: introducing myself in case they've
forgotten, even though we've been meeting like
this for years. I explain why I've come and ask
their permission to harvest, inquiring politely if
they would be willing to share.

Eating leeks is a spring tonic that blurs the line
between food and medicine. It wakens the body
from its winter lassitude and quickens the blood.
But I have another need, too, that only greens
from this particular woods can satisfy. Both of
my daughters will be home for the weekend from
the far places where they live. I ask these leeks to

renew the bonds between this ground and my
children, so that they will always carry the sub-
stance of home in the mineral of their bones.

Some of the leaves are already expanded –
stretching toward the sun – while others are still
rolled into a spear, thrusting up through the duff.
I dig my trowel in around the edge of the clump,
but they're deeply rooted and tightly packed,
resisting my efforts. It's just a small trowel and it
hurts my winter-softened hand, but at last I pry
out a clump and shake away the dark earth.

I expected a cluster of fat white bulbs, but in
their place I find ragged papery sheathes where
the bulbs should be. Withered and flaccid, they
look as if all the juice has already been sucked
out of them. Which it has. If you ask permission,
you have to listen to the answer. I tuck them
back in the soil and go home. Along the stone
wall, the elderberries have broken bud and their
embryonic leaves reach out like gloved purple
hands.

On a day like this, when the fiddleheads are
unfurling and the air is petal soft, I am awash
in longing. I know that 'thou shalt not covet thy

neighbor's chloroplasts' is good advice and yet I must confess to full-blown chlorophyll envy. Sometimes I wish I could photosynthesize so that just by being, just by shimmering at the meadow's edge or floating lazily on a pond, I could be doing the work of the world while standing silent in the sun. The shadowy hemlocks and the waving grasses are spinning out sugar molecules and passing them on to hungry mouths and mandibles all the while listening to the warblers and watching the light dance on the water.

It would be so satisfying to provide for the well-being of others – like being a mother again, like being needed. Shade, medicine, berries, roots; there would be no end to it. As a plant I could make the campfire, hold the nest, heal the wound, fill the brimming pot.

But this generosity is beyond my realm, as I am a mere heterotroph, a feeder on the carbon transmuted by others. In order to live, I must consume. That's the way the world works, the exchange of a life for a life, the endless cycling between my body and the body of the world. Forced to choose, I must admit I actually like my heterotroph role. Besides, if I could photosynthesize, I couldn't eat leeks.

So instead I live vicariously through the photosynthesis of others. I am not the vibrant leaves on the forest floor – I am the woman with the basket, and how I fill it is a question that matters. If we are fully awake, a moral question arises as we extinguish the other lives around us on behalf of our own. Whether we are digging wild leeks or going to the mall, how do we consume in a way that does justice to the lives that we take?

In our oldest stories, we are reminded that this was a question of profound concern for our ancestors. When we rely deeply on other lives, there is urgency to protect them. Our ancestors, who had so few material possessions, devoted a great deal of attention to this question, while we who are drowning in possessions scarcely give it a thought. The cultural landscape may have changed, but the conundrum has not – the need to resolve the inescapable tension between honoring life around us and taking it in order to live is part of being human.

A few weeks later I take up my basket and again

cross the field, still bare while the earth on the other side of the wall is drifted in snowy white trillium blossoms like a late-season snowfall. I must look like a ballet dancer tiptoeing and spinning between clumps of delicate Dutchman's-breeches, mysterious blue shoots of cohosh, patches of bloodroot, and the green shoots of jack-in-the-pulpit and mayapple surging up through the leaves. I greet them one by one and feel as if they're glad to see me, too.

We are told to take only that which is given, and when I was here last the leeks had nothing to give. Bulbs hold energy saved up for the next generation like money in the bank. Last fall the bulbs were sleek and fat, but, in the first days of spring, that savings account gets depleted as the roots send their stored energy into the emerging leaves to fuel their journey from soil to sunshine. In their first few days, the leaves are consumers, taking from the root, shriveling it up and giving nothing back. But as they unfurl they become a powerful solar array that will recharge the energy of the roots, playing out the reciprocity between consuming and producing in a few short weeks.

The leeks today are twice the size they were on my first visit and the scent of onions is strong where a deer has bruised the leaves. I pass by the first clump and kneel by the second. Once again, I quietly ask permission.

Asking permission shows respect for the personhood of the plant, but it is also an assessment of the well-being of the population. Thus I must use both sides of my brain to listen to the answer. The analytic left reads the empirical signs to judge whether the population is large and healthy enough to sustain a harvest, whether it has enough to share. The intuitive right hemisphere is reading something else, a sense of generosity, an open-handed radiance that says *take me*, or sometimes a tight-lipped recalcitrance that makes me put my trowel away. I can't explain it, but it is a kind of knowing that is for me just as compelling as a no-trespassing sign. This time, when I push my trowel deep I come up with a thick cluster of gleaming white bulbs, plump, slippery, and aromatic. I hear *yes*, so I make a gift from the soft old tobacco pouch in my pocket and begin to dig.

Leeks are clonal plants that multiply by

division, spreading the patch wider and wider. As a result, they tend to become crowded in the center of a patch, so I try to harvest there. In this way my taking can help the growth of the remaining plants by thinning them out. From camas bulbs to sweetgrass, blueberries to basket willow, our ancestors found ways to harvest that bring long-term benefit to plants and people.

While a sharp shovel would make digging more efficient, the truth is that it makes the work too fast. If I could get all the leeks I needed in five minutes, I'd lose that time on my knees watching the ginger poke up and listening to the oriole that has just returned home. This is truly a choice for 'slow food.' Besides, that simple shift in technology would also make it easy to slice through neighboring plants and take too much. Woods throughout the country are losing their leeks to harvesters who love them to extinction. The difficulty of digging is an important constraint. Not everything should be convenient.

The traditional ecological knowledge of indigenous harvesters is rich in prescriptions for sustainability. They are found in Native science and philosophy, in lifeways and practices, but most of all in stories, the ones that are told to help restore balance, to locate ourselves once again in the circle.

Anishinaabe elder Basil Johnston tells of the time our teacher Nanabozho was fishing in the lake for supper, as he often did, with hook and line. Heron came striding along through the reeds on his long, bent legs, his beak like a spear. Heron is a good fisherman and a sharing friend, so he told Nanabozho about a new way to fish that would make his life much easier. Heron cautioned him to be careful not to take too many fish, but Nanabozho was already thinking of a feast. He went out early the next day and soon had a whole basketful of fish, so heavy he could barely carry it and far more than he could eat. So he cleaned all those fish and set them out to dry on the racks outside his lodge. The next day, with his belly still full, he went back to the lake and again did what Heron had showed him. 'Aah,' he thought as he carried home the fish, 'I will have plenty to eat this winter.'

Day after day he stuffed himself and, as the lake grew empty, his drying racks grew full, sending out a delicious smell into the forest where Fox was licking his lips. Again he went to the lake, so proud of himself. But that day his nets came up empty and Heron looked down on him as he flew over the lake with a critical eye. When Nanabozho got home to his lodge, he learned a key rule – never take more than you need. The racks of fish were toppled in the dirt and every bite was gone.

Cautionary stories of the consequences of taking too much are ubiquitous in Native cultures, but it's hard to recall a single one in English. Perhaps this helps to explain why we seem to be caught in a trap of overconsumption, which is as destructive to ourselves as to those we consume.

Collectively, the indigenous canon of principles and practices that govern the exchange of life for life is known as the Honorable Harvest. They are rules of sorts that govern our taking, shape our relationships with the natural world, and rein in our tendency to consume – that the world might be as rich for the seventh generation as it is for our own. The details are highly specific to different cultures and ecosystems, but the fundamental principles are nearly universal among peoples who live close to the land.

I am a student of this way of thinking, not a scholar. As a human being who cannot photosynthesize, I must struggle to participate in the Honorable Harvest. So I lean in close to watch and listen to those who are far wiser than I am. What I share here, in the same way they were shared with me, are seeds gleaned from the fields of their collective wisdom, the barest surface, the moss on the mountain of their knowledge. I feel grateful for their teachings and responsible for passing them on as best I can.

My friend is the town clerk in a small Adirondack village. In the summer and fall there is a line outside her door for fishing and hunting licenses. With every laminated card, she hands out the harvesting regulations, pocket-size booklets on thin newsprint, printed in black and white except for glossy inserts with photos of the actual prey, just in case people don't know what they're shooting at. It happens: every year there is a story about triumphal deer hunters being stopped on the highway with a Jersey calf tied to their bumper.

A friend of mine once worked at a hunting check station during partridge season. A guy drove up in a big white Oldsmobile and proudly opened his trunk for inspection of his take. The birds were all neatly laid out on a canvas sheet, lined up beak to back with plumage scarcely ruffled, a whole brace of yellow-shafted flickers.

Traditional peoples who feed their families from the land have harvest guidelines too: detailed protocols designed to maintain the health and vigor of wildlife species. Like the state regulations, they too are based on sophisticated ecological knowledge and long-term monitoring of populations. They share the common goal of protecting what hunting managers call 'the resource,' both for its own sake and to safeguard the sustainable supply for future generations.

Early colonists on Turtle Island were stunned by the plenitude they found here, attributing the richness to the bounty of nature. Settlers in the Great Lakes wrote in their journals about the extraordinary abundance of wild rice harvested by Native peoples; in just a few days, they could fill their canoes with enough rice to last all year. But the settlers were puzzled by the fact that, as one of them wrote, 'the savages stopped gathering long before all the rice was harvested.' She observed that 'the rice harvest starts with a ceremony of thanksgiving and prayers for good weather for the next four days. They will harvest dawn till dusk for the prescribed four days and then stop, often leaving much rice to stand unreaped. This rice, they say, is not for them but for the Thunders. Nothing will compel them to continue, therefore much goes to waste.' The settlers took this as certain evidence of laziness and lack of industry on the part of the heathens. They did not understand how indigenous land-care practices might contribute to the wealth they encountered.

I once met an engineering student visiting from Europe who told me excitedly about going ricing in Minnesota with his friend's Ojibwe family. He was eager to experience a bit of Native American culture. They were on the lake by dawn and all day long they poled through the rice beds, knocking the ripe seed into the canoe. 'It didn't take long to collect quite a bit,' he reported, 'but it's not very efficient. At least half of the rice just falls in the water and they didn't seem to care. It's wasted.' As a gesture of thanks to his hosts, a traditional ricing family, he offered to design a grain capture system that could be attached to the gunwales of their canoes. He sketched it out for them, showing how his technique could get 85 percent more rice. His hosts listened respectfully, then said, 'Yes, we could get more that way. But it's got to seed itself for next year. And what we leave behind is not wasted. You know, we're not the only ones who like rice. Do you think the ducks would stop here if we took it all?' Our teachings tell us to never take more than half.

When my basket holds enough leeks for dinner, I head home. Walking back through the flowers, I see a whole patch of snakeroot spreading its glistening leaves, which reminds me of a story told by an herbalist I know. She taught me one of the cardinal rules of gathering plants: 'Never take the first plant you find, as it might be the last – and you want that first one to speak well of you to the others of her kind.' That's not too hard to do when you come upon a whole stream bank of coltsfoot, when there's a third and a fourth right behind the first, but it's harder when the plants are few and the desire is great.

'Once I dreamed of a snakeroot and that I should bring it with me on a journey the next day. There was a need but I didn't know what it was. But it was still too early to harvest. The leaves wouldn't be up for another week or so. There was a chance it might be up early somewhere – maybe in a sunny spot, so I went to look in the usual place I pick those medicines,' the herbalist recalled for me. The bloodroot was out and the spring beauties, too. She greeted them as she walked past, but saw none of the plant she sought. She stepped more slowly, opening her awareness, making her whole self into a halo of peripheral vision. Nestled at the base of a maple, on the southeast side, the snakeroot made itself visible, a glossy mass of dark-green leaves. She knelt, smiling, and spoke quietly. She thought of her upcoming journey, the empty bag in her pocket, and then slowly rose to her feet. Though her knees were stiff with age, she walked away, refraining from taking the first one.

She wandered through the woods, admiring the trillium just poking their heads up. And the leeks. But there was no more snakeroot. 'I just figured I'd have to do without. I was halfway home when I found I'd lost my little shovel, the one I always use for digging medicine. So I had to go back. Well, I found it all right – it's got a red handle so it's easy to find. And you know, it had fallen from my pocket right in a patch of root. So I talked to that plant, addressed it just like you would a person whose help you needed, and it gave me a bit of itself. When I got where I was going, sure enough, there was a woman there who needed that snakeroot medicine and I could pass on the gift. That plant reminded me that if we harvest with respect, the plants will help us.'

The guidelines for the Honorable Harvest are not written down, or even consistently spoken of as a whole – they are reinforced in small acts of daily life. But if you were to list them, they might look something like this:

Know the ways of the ones who take care of you,
*   so that you may take care of them.*
Introduce yourself. Be accountable as the one
*   who comes asking for life.*
Ask permission before taking. Abide by the
*   answer.*
Never take the first. Never take the last.
Take only what you need.
Take only that which is given.
Never take more than half. Leave some for
*   others.*
Harvest in a way that minimizes harm.
Use it respectfully. Never waste what you have
*   taken.*
Share.
Give thanks for what you have been given.
Give a gift, in reciprocity for what you have
*   taken.*
Sustain the ones who sustain you and the earth
*   will last forever.*

The state guidelines on hunting and gathering are based exclusively in the biophysical realm, while the rules of the Honorable Harvest are based on accountability to both the physical and the metaphysical worlds. The taking of another life to support your own is far more significant when you recognize the beings who are harvested as persons, nonhuman persons vested with awareness, intelligence, spirit – and who have families waiting for them at home. Killing a *who* demands something different than killing an *it*. When you regard those nonhuman persons as kinfolk, another set of harvesting regulations extends beyond bag limits and legal seasons.

The state regulations are, by and large, lists of illegal practices: 'It is unlawful to keep a rainbow trout whose length from snout to posterior fin does not exceed twelve inches.' The consequences for breaking the law are clearly stipulated and involve a financial transaction after a visit with your friendly conservation officer.

Unlike the state laws, the Honorable Harvest is not an enforced legal policy, but it is an agreement nonetheless, among people and most especially between consumers and providers. The providers have the upper hand. The deer, the sturgeon, the berries, and the leeks say, 'If you follow these rules, we will continue to give our lives so that you may live.'

Imagination is one of our most powerful tools. What we imagine, we can become. I like to imagine what it would be like if the Honorable Harvest were the law of the land today, as it was in our past. Imagine if a developer, eying open land for a shopping mall, had to ask the goldenrod, the meadowlarks, and the monarch butterflies for permission to take their homeland. What if he had to abide by the answer? Why not?

I like to imagine a laminated card, like the one my friend the town clerk hands out with the hunting and fishing licenses, embossed with the rules of the Honorable Harvest. Everyone would be subject to the same laws, since they are, after all, the dictates of the *real* government: the democracy of species, the laws of Mother Nature.

When I ask my elders about the ways our people lived in order to keep the world whole and healthy, I hear the mandate to take only what you need. But we human people, descendants of Nanabozho, struggle, as he did, with self-restraint. The dictum to take only what you need leaves a lot of room for interpretation when our needs get so tangled with our wants.

This gray area yields then to a rule more primal than need, an old teaching nearly forgotten now in the din of industry and technology. Deeply rooted in cultures of gratitude, this ancient rule is not just to take only what you need, but to take only that which is given.

At the level of human interactions, we already do this. It's what we teach our kids. If you're visiting your sweet grandma and she offers you homemade cookies on her favorite china plate, you know what to do. You accept them with many 'thank yous' and cherish the relationship reinforced by cinnamon and sugar. You gratefully take what has been given. But you wouldn't dream of breaking into her pantry and just taking all the cookies without invitation, grabbing her china plate for good measure. That would be at a minimum a breach of good manners, a betrayal of the loving relationship. What's more, your grandma would be heartbroken, and not inclined to bake more cookies for you any time soon.

As a culture, though, we seem unable to extend these good manners to the natural world. The dishonorable harvest has become a way of life – we take what doesn't belong to us and destroy it beyond repair: Onondaga Lake, the Alberta tar sands, the rainforests of Malaysia, the list is endless. They are gifts from our sweet Grandmother Earth, which we take without asking. How do we find the Honorable Harvest again?

If we're picking berries or gathering nuts, taking only what is given makes a lot of sense. They offer themselves and by taking them we fulfill our reciprocal responsibility. After all, the plants have made these fruits with the express purpose of our taking them, to disperse and plant. By our use of their gifts, both species prosper and life is magnified. But what about when something is taken without a clear avenue for mutual benefit, when someone is going to lose?

How can we distinguish between that which is given by the earth and that which is not? When does taking become outright theft? I think my elders would counsel that there is no one path, that each of us must find our own way. In my wandering with this question, I've found dead ends and clear openings. Discerning all that it might mean is like bushwhacking through dense undergrowth. Sometimes I get faint glimpses of a deer trail.

It is hunting season and we are sitting on the porch of the cookhouse at Onondaga on a hazy October day. The leaves are smoky gold and fluttering down while we listen to the men tell stories. Jake, with a red bandanna around his hair, gets everybody laughing with a story about Junior's never-fail turkey call. With his feet on the railing and black braid hanging over the back of his chair, Kent tells about following a blood trail over new-fallen snow, bear tracking, and the one that got away. For the most part they're young men with reputations to build, along with one elder.

In a Seventh Generation ball cap and a thin gray ponytail, Oren gets his turn at a story and leads us along with him, through thickets and down ravines to get to his favorite hunting spot.

Smiling in recollection, he says, 'I must have seen ten deer that day, but I only took one shot.' He tips his chair back and looks at the hill, remembering. The young men listen, looking intently at the porch floor. 'The first one came crunching through the dry leaves, but was shielded by the brush as it wove down the hill. It never saw me sitting there. Then a young buck came moving upwind toward me and then stepped behind a boulder. I could have tracked it and followed it across the crick, but I knew it wasn't the one.' Deer by deer, he recounts the day's encounters for which he never even raised his rifle: the doe by the water, the three-pointer concealed behind a basswood with only its rump showing. 'I only take one bullet with me,' he says.

The young men in T-shirts lean forward on the bench across from him. 'And then, without explanation, there's one who walks right into the clearing and looks you in the eye. He knows full well that you're there and what you're doing. He turns his flank right toward you for a clear shot. I know he's the one, and so does he. There's a kind of nod exchanged. That's why I only carry one shot. I wait for the one. He gave himself to me. That's what I was taught: take only what is given, and then treat it with respect.' Oren reminds his listeners, 'That's why we thank the deer as the leader of the animals, for its generosity in feeding the people. Acknowledging the lives that support ours and living in a way that demonstrates our gratitude is a force that keeps the world in motion.'

The Honorable Harvest does not ask us to photosynthesize. It does not say *don't take*, but offers inspiration and a model for what we *should* take. It's not so much a list of 'do not's' as a list of 'do's.' *Do* eat food that is honorably harvested, and celebrate every mouthful. *Do* use technologies that minimize harm; *do* take what is given. This philosophy guides not only our taking of food, but also any taking of the gifts of Mother Earth – air, water, and the literal body of the earth: the rocks and soil and fossil fuels.

Taking coal buried deep in the earth, for which we must inflict irreparable damage, violates every precept of the code. By no stretch of the imagination is coal 'given' to us. We have to wound the land and water to gouge it from

Mother Earth. What if a coal company planning mountaintop removal in the ancient folds of the Appalachians were compelled by law to take only that which is given? Don't you long to hand them the laminated card and announce that the rules have changed?

It doesn't mean that we can't consume the energy we need, but it does mean that we honorably take only what is given. The wind blows every day, every day the sun shines, every day the waves roll against the shore, and the earth is warm below us. We can understand these renewable sources of energy as given to us, since they are the sources that have powered life on the planet for as long as there has been a planet. We need not destroy the earth to make use of them. Solar, wind, geothermal, and tidal energy – the so-called 'clean energy' harvests – when they are wisely used seem to me to be consistent with the ancient rules of the Honorable Harvest.

And the code might ask of any harvest, including energy, that our purpose be worthy of the harvest. Oren's deer made moccasins and fed three families. What will we use our energy for?

I once gave a lecture titled 'Cultures of Gratitude' at a small private college where tuition ran upwards of $40,000 a year. For the allocated fifty-five minutes, I talked about the Thanksgiving Address of the Haudenosaunee, the potlatch tradition of the Pacific Northwest, and the gift economies of Polynesia. Then I told a traditional story of the years when the corn harvests were so plentiful that the caches were full. The fields had been so generous with the villagers that the people scarcely needed to work. So they didn't. Hoes leaned against a tree, idle. The people became so lazy that they let the time for corn ceremonies go by without a single song of gratitude. They began to use the corn in ways the Three Sisters had not intended when they gave the people corn as a sacred gift of food. They burned it for fuel when they couldn't be bothered to cut firewood. The dogs dragged it off from the untidy heaps the people made instead of storing the harvest in secure granaries. No one stopped the kids when they kicked ears around the village in their games.

Saddened by the lack of respect, the Corn Spirit

decided to leave, to go where she would be appreciated. At first the people didn't even notice. But the next year, the cornfields were nothing but weeds. The caches were nearly empty and the grain that had been left untended was moldy and mouse-chewed. There was nothing to eat. The people sat about in despair, growing thinner and thinner. When they abandoned gratitude, the gifts abandoned them.

One small child walked out from the village and wandered for hungry days until he found the Corn Spirit in a sunlit clearing in the woods. He begged her to return to his people. She smiled kindly at him and instructed him to teach his people the gratitude and respect that they had forgotten. Only then would she return. He did as she asked and after a hard winter without corn, to remind them of the cost, she returned to them in the spring.*

Several students in my audience yawned. They

* This story is known from the southwest to the northeast. One version is told by Joseph Bruchac, in Caduto and Bruchac's *Keepers of Life*.

could not imagine such a thing. The aisles of the grocery store were always well stocked. At a reception afterward the students filled their Styrofoam plates with the usual fare. We exchanged questions and comments while we balanced plastic cups of punch. The students grazed on cheese and crackers, a profusion of cut vegetables, and buckets of dip. There was enough food to feast a small village. The leftovers were swept into trash bins placed conveniently next to the tables.

A beautiful young girl, dark hair tied up in a headscarf, was hanging back from the discussion, waiting her turn. When nearly everyone had left she approached me, gesturing with an apologetic smile at the wasted remains of the reception. 'I don't want you to think no one understands what you were saying,' she said. 'I do. You sound like my grandmother, back in my village in Turkey. I will tell her she must have a sister here in the United States. The Honorable Harvest is her way, too. In her house, we learned that everything we put in our mouths, everything that allows us to live, is the gift of another life. I remember lying with her at night as she made us thank the rafters of her house and the wool blankets we slept in. My grandma wouldn't let us forget that these are all gifts, which is why you take care of everything, to show respect for that life. In my grandmother's house we were taught to kiss the rice. If a single grain fell to the ground, we learned to pick it up and kiss it, to show we meant no disrespect in wasting it.' The student told me that, when she came to the United States, the greatest culture shock she experienced was not language or food or technology, but waste.

'I've never told anyone before,' she said, 'but the cafeteria made me sick, because of the way people treated their food. What people throw away here after one lunch would supply my village for days. I could not speak to anyone of this; no one else would understand to kiss the grain of rice.' I thanked her for her story and she said, 'Please, take it as a gift, and give it to someone else.'

I've heard it said that sometimes, in return for the gifts of the earth, gratitude is enough. It is our uniquely human gift to express thanks, because we have the awareness and the collective memory to remember that the world could well be otherwise, less generous than it is. But I think we are called to go beyond cultures of gratitude, to once again become cultures of reciprocity.

I met Carol Crowe, an Algonquin ecologist, at a meeting on indigenous models of sustainability. She told the story of requesting funding from her tribal council to attend the conference. They asked her, 'What is this all about, this notion of sustainability? What are they talking about?' She gave them a summary of the standard definitions of sustainable development, including 'the management of natural resources and social institutions in such a manner as to ensure the attainment and continued satisfaction of human needs for present and future generations.' They were quiet for a while, considering. Finally one elder said, 'This sustainable development sounds to me like they just want to be able to keep on taking like they always have. It's always about taking. You go there and tell them that in our way, our first thoughts are not 'What can we take? ' but 'What can we give to Mother Earth?' That's how it's supposed to be.'

53

The Honorable Harvest asks us to give back, in reciprocity, for what we have been given. Reciprocity helps resolve the moral tension of taking a life by giving in return something of value that sustains the ones who sustain us. One of our responsibilities as human people is to find ways to enter into reciprocity with the more-than-human world. We can do it through gratitude, through ceremony, through land stewardship, science, art, and in everyday acts of practical reverence.

I have to confess that I'd shuttered my mind before I even met him. There was nothing a fur trapper could say that I wanted to hear. Berries, nuts, leeks, and, arguably, that deer who looks you in the eye, are all part of the matrix of the Honorable Harvest, but laying snares for snowy ermine and soft-footed lynx in order to adorn wealthy women is hard to justify. But I would certainly be respectful and listen.

Lionel grew up in the north woods, hunting, fishing, guiding, making a living off the land in a remote log cabin, carrying on the tradition of the *coureurs des bois*. He learned trapping from his

Indian grandfather who was renowned for his skills on the trapline. To catch a mink, you have to be able to think like a mink. His grandpa was a successful trapper because of his deep respect for the knowledge of the animals, where they traveled, how they hunted, where they would den up in bad weather. He could see the world through ermine eyes and so provided for his family.

'I loved living in the bush,' Lionel says, 'and I loved the animals.' Fishing and hunting gave the family their food; the trees gave them heat; and after their needs for warm hats and mittens were provided for, the furs they sold every year gave them cash for kerosene, coffee, beans, and school clothes. It was assumed that he would follow in the trade, but as a young man he refused. He wanted nothing more of trapping in the years when leg-hold traps became the norm. It was a cruel technology. He'd seen the animals who gnawed off their feet to free themselves. 'Animals do have to die for us to live, but they don't have to suffer,' he says.

To stay in the bush he tried logging. He was practiced in the old methods for sledding out timber in the winter along an ice road, felling while the snow blanket protected the earth. But the old, low-impact practices had given way to big machines that ripped up the forest and wrecked the land his animals needed. The dark forest turned to ragged stumps, the clear streams to muddy trenches. He tried to work in the cab of the D9 Cat, and a feller-buncher, a machine designed to take it all. But he couldn't do it.

Then Lionel went to work in the mines at Sudbury, Ontario, left the woods to work underground, digging nickel ore from the earth to be fed into the maw of furnaces. Sulfur dioxide and heavy metals poured from the stacks, making a toxic acid rain that killed every living thing for miles, a gigantic burn mark on the land. Without vegetation, the soil all washed away, leaving a moonscape so bare that NASA used it to test lunar vehicles. The metal smelters at Sudbury held the earth in a leg-hold trap, and the forest was dying a slow and painful death. Too late, after the damage was done, Sudbury became the poster child for clean-air legislation.

There is no shame in working the mines to feed

your family – an exchange of hard labor in return for food and shelter – but you want your labor to count for something more. Driving home each night through the moonscape his labor created, he felt blood on his hands, and so he quit.

Today Lionel spends his winter days on snowshoes on his trapline and winter nights preparing furs. Unlike the harsh chemicals of the factory, brain tanning yields the softest, most durable hide. He says with wonder in his voice and a soft moose hide on his lap, 'There is just enough in each animal's brain to tan its own hide.' His own brain and his heart led him back home to the woods.

Lionel is of the Métis Nation; he calls himself 'a blue-eyed Indian,' raised in the deep woods of northern Quebec, as his melodious accent suggests. His conversation is so delightfully sauced with '*Oui, oui, madame*' that I imagine he will kiss my hand at any moment. His own hands are telling: woodsman's hands broad and strong enough to set a trap or a logging chain but sensitive enough to stroke a pelt to gauge its thickness. By the time we spoke, leg-hold traps had been banned in Canada and only body-hold traps that ensure a sudden death were permitted. He demonstrates one: it takes two strong arms to open and set, and its powerful snap would break a neck in an instant.

Trappers spend more time on the land than anyone else these days, and they maintain detailed records of their harvest. Lionel keeps a thickly penciled notebook in his vest pocket; he takes it out and waves it, saying, 'Wanna see my new BlackBerry? I just download my data to my bush computer, runs on propane, don't you know.'

His traplines yield beaver, lynx, coyote, fisher, mink, and ermine. He runs his hand over the pelts, explaining about the density of the winter undercoat and the long guard hairs, how you can judge the health of an animal by its fur. He pauses when he comes to martens, whose pelage is legendary in its silky-soft luxury – the American sable. It is beautifully colored and feather light.

Martens are part of Lionel's life here – they're his neighbors and he is thankful that they have rebounded from near extirpation. Trappers like him are on the front line of monitoring wildlife populations and well-being. They have a responsibility to take care of the species they rely upon, and every visit to the trapline produces data that govern the trapper's response. 'If we catch only male martens, we will keep the traps open,' he says. When there is an excess of unpaired males, they are wandering and easy to trap. Too many young males can leave less food for the others. 'But as soon as we get a female, we stop trapping. That means we've skimmed off the excess and we don't touch the rest. That way the population doesn't get too crowded, none will go hungry, but their population will continue to grow.'

In late winter, when the snow is still heavy but the days are lengthening, Lionel drags down the ladder from the rafters in his garage. He straps on his snowshoes and stomps out into the bush with the ladder on his shoulder and hammer, nails, and scrap wood in his pack basket. He scouts out just the right spots: big old trees with cavities are best, as long as the size and shape of the hole dictates that only a single species can use it. He climbs to where the ladder, anchored in the snow, leans against a high branch and he constructs a platform. He makes it home before dark and rises the next day to do it again. It's hard work lugging a ladder through the woods. When he's done with the platforms, he pulls a white plastic pail from the freezer and sets it by the woodstove to thaw.

All summer long Lionel serves as a fishing guide on the remote lakes and rivers of his birth. He jokes that he works for only himself now and he calls his company See More and Do Less. Not a bad business plan. When he and his 'sports' clean their catch he scrapes the guts into big white pails and keeps them in his freezer. He overheard his clients whispering, 'Must be he eats fish-gut stew in the winter.'

The next day he's off again, pulling the bucket on a sled, miles down the trapline. At every platform tree, he scrambles up the ladder, with somewhat less grace than a weasel, one-handed. (You don't want to slop fish guts all over yourself.) He shovels out a big smelly scoop onto each platform and then hikes off to the next.

Like many predators, martens are slow reproducers, which makes them vulnerable to decline, especially when they're exploited. Gestation is about nine months, and they don't give birth until they're three years old. They'll have from one to four young and raise only as many as the food supply allows. 'I put out the gut piles in the last weeks before the little mothers give birth,' Lionel says. 'If you put them where nothing else can get them, those mothers will have some extra-good meals. That will help them to nurse their babies so more will survive, especially if we get a late snow or something.' The tenderness in his voice makes me think of a neighbor delivering a warm casserole to a shut-in. It's not how I've thought of trappers. 'Well,' he says, blushing a little, 'dose little martens take care of me and I take care of dem.'

The teachings tell us that a harvest is made honorable by what you give in return for what you take. There is no escaping the fact that Lionel's care will result in more martens on his trapline. There is no escaping the fact that they will also be killed. Feeding mama martens is not altruism; it is deep respect for the way the world works, for the connections between us, of life flowing into life. The more he gives, the more he can take, and he goes the extra mile to give more than he takes.

I'm moved by Lionel's affection and respect for these animals, for the care that flows from his intimate knowledge of their needs. He lives the tension of loving his prey and resolves it for himself by practicing the tenets of the Honorable Harvest. But there is also no escaping the fact that the marten pelts are likely to become a luxury coat for a very wealthy person, perhaps the owner of the Sudbury mine.

These animals will die by his hand, but first they will live well, in part by his hand. His lifestyle, which I had condemned without understanding, protects the forest, protects the lakes and rivers, not just for him and the furbearers, but for all the forest beings. A harvest is made honorable when it sustains the giver as well as the taker. And today Lionel is also a gifted teacher, invited to schools far and wide to share his traditional knowledge of wildlife and conservation. He is giving back what was given to him.

It's hard for the guy wearing the sable in the

corner office of Sudbury to imagine Lionel's world, to even conceive of a way of living that would require him to consider taking only what he needs, to give back in reciprocity for what he takes, to nurture the world that nurtures him, to carry meals to a nursing mother in a wild tree-top den. But unless we want more wastelands, he needs to learn.

These may seem like charming anachronisms, rules for hunting and gathering whose relevance vanished along with the buffalo. But remember that the buffalo are not extinct and in fact are making a resurgence under the care of those who remember. The canon of the Honorable Harvest is poised to make its comeback, too, as people remember that what's good for the land is also good for the people.

We need acts of restoration, not only for polluted waters and degraded lands, but also for our relationship to the world. We need to restore honor to the way we live, so that when we walk through the world we don't have to avert our eyes with shame, so that we can hold our heads up high and receive the respectful acknowledgment of the rest of the earth's beings.

I feel lucky to have wild leeks, dandelion greens, marsh marigolds, and hickory nuts – if I get there before the squirrels do. But these are decorations on a diet that comes mostly from my garden and from the grocery store, like everyone else, especially now that more people live in urban centers than the countryside.

Cities are like the mitochondria in our animal cells – they are consumers, fed by the autotrophs, the photosynthesis of a distant green landscape. We could lament that urban dwellers have little means of exercising direct reciprocity with the land. Yet while city folks may be separated from the sources of what they consume, they can exercise reciprocity through how they spend their money. While the digging of the leeks and the digging of the coal may be too far removed to see, we consumers have a potent tool of reciprocity right in our pockets. We can use our dollars as the indirect currency of reciprocity.

Perhaps we can think of the Honorable Harvest as a mirror by which we judge our purchases.

What do we see in the mirror? A purchase worthy of the lives consumed? Dollars become a surrogate, a proxy for the harvester with hands in the earth, and they can be used in support of the Honorable Harvest – or not.

It's easy to make this argument, and I believe that the principles of the Honorable Harvest have great resonance in an era when overconsumption threatens every dimension of our well-being. But it can be too easy to shift the burden of responsibility to the coal company or the land developers. What about me, the one who buys what they sell, who is complicit in the dishonorable harvest?

I live in the country, where I grow a big garden, get eggs from my neighbor's farm, buy apples from the next valley over, pick berries and greens from my few rewilding acres. A lot of what I own is secondhand, or third. The desk that I'm writing on was once a fine dining table that someone set out on the curb. But while I heat with wood, compost and recycle, and do myriad other responsible things, if I did an honest inventory of my household, most of it would probably not make the grade of the Honorable Harvest.

I want to do the experiment, to see if one can subsist in this market economy and still practice the rules of the Honorable Harvest. So I take my shopping list and go forth.

Actually, our local grocery store makes it pretty easy to be mindful of the choices and the mantra of mutual benefit for land and people. They've partnered with farmers for local organic goods at a price normal people can afford. They're big on 'green' and recycled products, too, so I can hold my toilet paper purchase up to the mirror of the Honorable Harvest without flinching. When I walk the aisles with open eyes, the source of the food is mostly evident, although Cheetos and Ding Dongs remain an ecological mystery. For the most part, I can use dollars as the currency of good ecological choices, alongside my questionable but persistent need for chocolate.

I don't have much patience with food proselytizers who refuse all but organic, free-range, fair-trade gerbil milk. We each do what we can; the Honorable Harvest is as much about the relationships as about the materials. A friend of mine says she buys just one green item a week – that's all she can do, so she does it. 'I want to vote with my dollar,' she says. I can make choices because I have the disposable income to choose 'green' over less-expensive goods, and I hope that will drive the market in the right direction. In the food deserts of the South Side there is no such choice, and the dishonor in that inequity runs far deeper than the food supply.

I am stopped in my tracks in the produce section. There on a Styrofoam tray, sheathed in plastic and tagged at the princely sum of $15.50 per pound, are Wild Leeks. The plastic presses down on them: they look trapped and suffocated. Alarm bells go off in my head, alarms of commoditization of what should be regarded as a gift and all the dangers that follow from that kind of thinking. Selling leeks makes them into mere objects and cheapens them, even at $15.50 per pound. Wild things should not be for sale.

Next stop is the mall, a place I try to avoid at all costs, but today I will go into the belly of the beast in service to my experiment. I sit in the car for a few minutes trying to rouse the same attunement and outlook with which I go to the woods, receptive, observant, and grateful, but I'll be gathering a new stock of paper and pens instead of wild leeks.

There is a stone wall to cross here, too, the three-story edifice of the mall, bordered by another lifeless field of parking lot, with crows perched on the stanchions. As I cross the wall, the floor is hard beneath my feet and heels click on the faux-marble tile. I pause to take in the sounds. Inside, there are neither crows nor wood thrushes, but rather a soundtrack of strangely sanitized oldies set to strings, hovering above the drone of the ventilation system. The light is dim fluorescent with spotlights to dapple the floor, the better to highlight the splashes of color which identify the shops, their logos as readily identifiable as patches of bloodroot across the forest. Like in the spring woods, the air is a patchwork of scents that I walk among: coffee here, cinnamon buns there, a shop of scented candles, and beneath it all the pervasive tang of fast-food Chinese from the food court.

At the end of the wing, I spy the habitat of my quarry. I navigate easily, as I've been coming here for years for my traditional harvest of writing supplies. At the store entrance is a stack of bright red plastic shopping bins with metal handles. I pick one up and again become the woman with the basket. In the paper aisle I am confronted with a great diversity of species of paper – wide ruled and narrow, copier paper, stationery, spiral bound, loose-leaf – arrayed in clonal patches by brand and purpose. I see just what I want, my favorite legal pads, as yellow as a downy violet.

I stand before them trying to conjure the gathering mentality, to bring all the rules of the Honorable Harvest to bear, but I can't do it without the bite of mockery. I try to sense the trees in that stack of paper and address my thoughts to them, but the taking of their lives is so far removed from this shelf that there is just a distant echo. I think about the harvesting method: were they clear-cut? I think about the stink of the paper mill, the effluent, the dioxin. Fortunately, there is a stack labeled 'Recycled,' so I choose those, paying a little more for the privilege. I pause and consider whether the yellow dyed may be worse than the white bleached. I have my suspicions, but I choose the yellow as I always do. It looks so nice with green or purple ink, like a garden.

I wander next to the pen aisle, or as they call it, 'writing instruments.' The choices here are even more numerous and I have no idea at all where they came from, except some petrochemical synthesis. How can I bring honor to this purchase, use my dollars as the currency of honor when the lives behind the product are invisible? I stand there so long that an 'associate' comes to ask if I'm looking for anything in particular. I guess I look like a shoplifter planning a heist of 'writing instruments' with my little red basket. I'd like to ask him, 'Where did these things come from? What are they made of and which one was made with a technology that inflicts minimal damage on the earth? Can I buy pens with the same mentality with which a person digs wild leeks?' But I suspect he would call security on the little earpiece attached to his jaunty store cap, so I just choose my favorite, for the feel of the nib against the paper and the purple and green ink. At the checkout I engage in reciprocity, tendering my credit card in return for writing supplies. Both the clerk and I say thank you, but not to the trees.

I'm trying hard to make this work, but what I feel in the woods, the pulsing animacy, is simply not here. I realize why the tenets of reciprocity don't work here, why this glittering labyrinth seems to make a mockery of the Honorable Harvest. It's so obvious, but I didn't see it, so intent was I on searching for the lives behind the products. I couldn't find them because the lives aren't here. Everything for sale here is dead.

I get a cup of coffee and sit on a bench to watch the scene unfold, gathering evidence as best I can, notebook open in my lap. Sullen teenagers wanting to buy their selfhood and sad-looking old men sitting alone at the food court. Even the plants are plastic. I've never been shopping like this before, with such intentional awareness of what goes on here. I suppose I've blocked it out in my usual hurry to get in, make my purchase, and get out. But now I scan the landscape with all senses heightened. Open to the T-shirts, the plastic earrings, and the iPods. Open to shoes that hurt, delusions that hurt, and mountains of needless stuff that hurts the chances that my grandchildren will have a good green earth to care for. It hurts me even to bring the ideas of the Honorable Harvest here; I feel protective of them. I want to cup them like a small warm animal in my hands and shelter them from the onslaught of their antithesis. But I know they are stronger than this.

It's not the Honorable Harvest that is the aberration, though – it is this marketplace. As leeks cannot survive in a cutover forest, the Honorable Harvest cannot survive in this habitat. We have constructed an artifice, a Potemkin village of an ecosystem where we perpetrate the illusion that the things we consume have just fallen off the back of Santa's sleigh, not been ripped from the earth. The illusion enables us to imagine that the only choices we have are between brands.

Back home I wash away the last bits of black soil and trim the long white roots. One big handful of leeks we set aside, unwashed. The girls chop the slender bulbs and the leaves, and they all go into my favorite cast iron skillet with way more butter than a person should probably have. The aroma of sautéed leeks fills the kitchen. Just breathing it in is good medicine. The sharp pungency dissipates quickly and the fragrance that lingers is deep and savory, with a hint of leaf mold and rainwater. Potato leek soup, wild leek risotto, or just a bowl of leeks are nourishment for body and soul. When my daughters leave on Sunday, I'm happy to know that something of their childhood woods will travel with them.

After dinner, I take the basket of unwashed leeks to the tiny patch of forest above my pond to plant them. The harvesting process now unfolds in reverse. I ask permission to bring them here, to open the earth for their arrival. I search out the rich moist hollows and tuck them into the soil, emptying my basket instead of filling it. These woods are second or third growth and sadly lost their leeks long ago. It turns out that when forests around here grow back after agricultural clearing, the trees come back readily but the understory plants do not.

From a distance the new postagricultural woods look healthy; the trees came back thick and strong. But inside something is missing. The April showers do not bring May flowers. No trillium, no mayapple, no bloodroot. Even after a century of regrowth, the postfarming forests are impoverished, while the untilled forests just across the wall are an explosion of blossoms. The medicines are missing, for reasons ecologists do not yet understand. It might be microhabitat, it might be dispersal, but it is clear that the original habitat for these old medicines was obliterated in a cascade of unintended consequences as the land was turned to corn. The land is no longer hospitable for the medicines and we don't know why.

The Skywoman woods across the valley have never been plowed, so they still have their full glory, but most other woods are missing their forest floor. Leek-laden woods have become a rarity. Left to time and chance alone, my cutover woods would probably never recover their leeks or their trillium. The way I see it, it's up to me to carry them over the wall. Over the years, this replanting on my hillside has yielded small patches of vibrant green in April and nurtures the hope that the leeks can return to their homelands and that when I'm an old lady I'll have a celebratory spring supper close at hand. They give to me, I give to them. Reciprocity is an investment in abundance for both the eater and the eaten.

We need the Honorable Harvest today. But like the leeks and the marten, it is an endangered species that arose in another landscape, another time, from a legacy of traditional knowledge. That ethic of reciprocity was cleared away along with the forests, the beauty of justice traded away for more stuff. We've created a cultural and economic landscape that is hospitable to the growth of neither leeks nor honor. If the earth is nothing more than inanimate matter, if lives are nothing more than commodities, then the way of the Honorable Harvest, too, is dead. But when you stand in the stirring spring woods, you know otherwise.

It is an animate earth that we hear calling to us to feed the martens and kiss the rice. Wild leeks and wild ideas are in jeopardy. We have to transplant them both and nurture their return to the lands of their birth. We have to carry them across the wall, restoring the Honorable Harvest, bringing back the medicine.

People of Corn, People of Light

The story of our relationship to the earth is written more truthfully on the land than on the page. It lasts there. The land remembers what we said and what we did. Stories are among our most potent tools for restoring the land as well as our relationship to land. We need to unearth the old stories that live in a place and begin to create new ones, for we are storymakers, not just storytellers. All stories are connected, new ones woven from the threads of the old. One of the ancestor stories, that waits for us to listen again with new ears, is the Mayan story of Creation.

It is said that in the beginning there was emptiness. The divine beings, the great thinkers, imagined the world into existence simply by saying its name.

The world was populated with a rich flora and fauna, called into being by words. But the divine beings were not satisfied. Among the wonderful beings they had created, none were articulate. They could sing and squawk and growl, but none had voice to tell the story of their creation nor praise it. So the gods set about to make humans.

The first humans, the gods shaped of mud. But the gods were none too happy with the result. The people were not beautiful; they were ugly and ill formed. They could not talk – they could barely walk and certainly could not dance or sing the praises of the gods. They were so crumbly and clumsy and inadequate that they could not even reproduce and just melted away in the rain.

So the gods tried again to make good people who would be givers of respect, givers of praise, providers and nurturers. To this end they carved a man from wood and a woman from the pith of a reed. Oh, these were beautiful people, lithe and strong; they could talk and dance and sing. Clever people, too: they learned to use the other beings, plants and animals, for their own purposes. They made many things, farms and pottery and houses, and nets to catch fish. As a result of their fine bodies and fine minds and hard work, these people reproduced and populated the world, filling it with their numbers.

But after a time the all-seeing gods realized that these people's hearts were empty of compassion and love. They could sing and talk, but their words were without gratitude for the sacred gifts that they had received. These clever people did not know thanks or caring and so endangered the rest of the Creation. The gods wished to end this failed experiment in humanity and so they sent great catastrophes to the world – they sent a flood, and earthquakes, and, most importantly, they loosed the retaliation of the other species. The previously mute trees and fish and clay were given voices for their grief and anger at the disrespect shown them by the humans made of wood. Trees raged against the humans for their sharp axes, the deer for their arrows, and even the pots made of earthen clay rose up in anger for the times they had been carelessly burnt. All of the misused members of Creation rallied together and destroyed the people made of wood in self-defense. Once again the gods tried to make human beings, but this time purely of light, the sacred energy of the sun. These humans were dazzling to behold, seven times the color of the sun, beautiful, smart, and very, very powerful. They knew so much that they believed they knew everything. Instead of being grateful to the creators

*for their gifts, they believed themselves to be the gods'
equals. The divine beings understood the danger posed
by these people made of light and once more arranged
for their demise. And so the gods tried again to fashion
humans who would live right in the beautiful world
they had created, in respect and gratitude and humility. From two baskets of corn, yellow and white, they
ground a fine meal, mixed it with water, and shaped a
people made of corn. They were fed on corn liquor and
oh these were good people. They could dance and sing
and they had words to tell stories and offer up prayers.
Their hearts were filled with compassion for the rest of
Creation. They were wise enough to be grateful. The
gods had learned their lesson, so to protect the corn
people from the overpowering arrogance of their pre-
decessors, the people made of light, they passed a veil
before the eyes of the corn people, clouding their vision
as breath clouds a mirror. These people of corn are the
ones who were respectful and grateful for the world
that sustained them – and so they were the people who
were sustained upon the earth.**

Of all the materials, why is it that people of

---

* Adapted from oral tradition.

corn would inherit the earth, rather than people of mud or wood or light? Could it be that people made of corn are beings transformed? For what is corn, after all, but light transformed by relationship? Corn owes its existence to all four elements: earth, air, fire, and water. And corn is the product of relationship not only with the physical world, but with people too. The sacred plant of our origin created people, and people created corn, a great agricultural innovation from its teosinthe ancestor. Corn cannot exist without us to sow it and tend its growth; our beings are joined in an obligate symbiosis. From these reciprocal acts of creation arise the elements that were missing from the other attempts to create sustainable humanity: gratitude, and a capacity for reciprocity. I've read and loved this story as a history of sorts – a recounting of how, in long-ago times just at the edge of knowing, people were made of maize and lived happily ever after. But in many indigenous ways of knowing, time is not a river, but a lake in which the past, the present, and the future exist. Creation, then, is an ongoing process and the story is not history alone – it is also prophecy. Have we already become people of corn? Or are we still people made of wood? Are we people made of light, in thrall to our own power? Are we not yet transformed by relationship to earth? Perhaps this story could be a user's manual for understanding how we become people of corn. The Popul Vuh, the Mayan sacred text in which this story is contained, is perceived as more than just a chronicle.

As David Suzuki notes in *The Wisdom of the Elders,* the Mayan stories are understood as an *ilbal* – a precious seeing instrument, or lens, with which to view our sacred relationships. He suggests that such stories may offer us a corrective lens. But while our indigenous stories are rich in wisdom, and we need to hear them, I do not advocate their wholesale appropriation. As the world changes, an immigrant culture must write its own new stories of relationship to place – a new *ilbal,* but tempered by the wisdom of those who were old on this land long before we came. So how, then, can science, art, and story give us a new lens to understand the relationship that people made of corn represent? Someone once said that sometimes a fact alone is a poem. Just so, the people of corn are embedded in a beautiful poem, written in the language of chemistry. The first stanza goes like this: Carbon dioxide plus water combined in the presence of light and chlorophyll in the beautiful membrane-bound machinery of life yields sugar and oxygen. Photosynthesis, in other words, in which air, light, and water are combined out of nothingness into sweet morsels of sugar – the stuff of redwoods and daffodils and corn. Straw spun to gold, water turned to wine, photosynthesis is the link between the inorganic realm and the living world, making the inanimate live. At the same time it gives us oxygen. Plants give us food and breath. Here is the second stanza, the same as the first, but recited backward: Sugar combined with oxygen in the beautiful membrane-bound machinery of life called the mitochondria yields us right back where we began – carbon dioxide and water. Respiration – the source of energy that lets us farm and dance and speak. The breath of plants gives life to animals and the breath of animals gives life to plants. My breath is your breath, your breath is mine. It's the great poem of give and take, of reciprocity that animates the world. Isn't that a story worth telling? Only when people understand the symbiotic relationships that sustain them can they become people of corn, capable of gratitude and reciprocity. The very facts of the world *are* a poem. Light is turned to sugar. Salamanders find their way to ancestral ponds following magnetic lines radiating from the earth. The saliva of grazing buffalo causes the grass to grow taller. Tobacco seeds germinate when they smell smoke. Microbes in industrial waste can destroy mercury. Aren't these stories we should all know? Who is it who holds them? In long- ago times, it was the elders who carried them. In the twenty-first century, it is often scientists who first hear them. The stories of buffalo and salamanders belong to the land, but scientists are one of their translators and carry a large responsibility for conveying their stories to the world.And yet scientists mostly convey these stories in a language that excludes readers. Conventions for efficiency and precision make reading scientific papers very difficult for the rest of the world, and if the truth be known, for us as well. This has serious consequences for public dialogue about the environment and therefore for real democracy, especially the democracy of all species. For what good is knowing, unless it is coupled with caring? Science can give us knowing, but caring comes from someplace else. I think it's fair to say that if the Western world has an *ilbal,* it is science. Science lets us see the dance of the chromosomes, the leaves of moss, and the farthest galaxy. But is it a sacred lens like the Popul Vuh? Does science allow us to perceive the sacred in the world, or does it bend light in such a way as to obscure it? A lens that brings the material world into focus but blurs the spiritual is the lens of a people made of wood. It is not more data that we need for our transformation to people of corn, but more wisdom. While science could be a source of and repository for knowledge, the scientific worldview is all too often an enemy of ecological compassion. It is important in thinking about this lens to separate two ideas that are too often synonymous in the mind of the public: the practice of science and the scientific worldview that it feeds. Science is the process of revealing the world through rational inquiry. The practice of doing real science brings the questioner into an unparalleled intimacy with nature fraught with wonder and creativity as we try to comprehend the mysteries of the more-than-human world. Trying to understand the life of another being or another system so unlike our own is often humbling and, for many scientists, is a deeply spiritual pursuit. Contrasting with this is the scientific worldview, in which a culture uses the process of interpreting science in a cultural context that uses science and technology to reinforce reductionist, materialist economic and political agendas. I maintain that the destructive lens of the people made of wood is not science itself, but the lens of the scientific worldview, the illusion of dominance and control, the separation of knowledge from responsibility. I dream of a world guided by a lens of stories rooted in the revelations of science and framed with an indigenous worldview – stories in which matter and spirit are both given voice. Scientists are particularly good at learning about the lives of other species. The stories they could tell convey the intrinsic values of the lives of other beings, lives every bit as interesting, maybe more so, as those of *Homo sapiens*. But while scientists are among those who are privy to these other intelligences, many seem to believe that the intelligence they access is only their own. They lack the fundamental ingredient: humility. After the gods experimented with arrogance, they gave the people of corn humility, and it takes humility to learn from other species. In the indigenous view, humans are viewed as somewhat lesser beings in the democracy of species. We are referred to as the younger brothers of Creation, so like younger brothers we must learn from our elders. Plants were here first and have had a long time to figure things out. They live both above and below ground and hold the earth in place. Plants know how to make food from light and water. Not only do they feed themselves, but they make enough to sustain the lives of all the rest of us. Plants are providers for the rest of the community and exemplify the virtue of generosity, always offering food. What if Western scientists saw plants as their teachers rather than their subjects? What if they told stories with that lens? Many indigenous peoples share the understanding that we are each endowed with a particular gift, a unique ability. Birds to sing and stars to glitter, for instance. It is understood that these gifts have a dual nature, though: a gift is also a responsibility. If the bird's gift is song, then it has a responsibility to greet the day with music. It is the duty of birds to sing and the rest of us receive the song as a gift. Asking what is our responsibility is perhaps also to ask, What is our gift? And how shall we use it? Stories like the one about the people of corn give us guidance, both to recognize the world as a gift and to think how we might respond. The people of mud and wood and light all lacked gratitude and the sense of reciprocity that flowed from it. It was only the people of corn, people transformed by awareness of their gifts and responsibilities, who were sustained on the earth. Gratitude comes first, but gratitude alone is not enough. Other beings are known to be especially gifted, with attributes that humans lack. Other beings can fly, see at night, rip open trees with their claws, make maple syrup. What can humans do? We may not have wings or leaves, but we humans do have words. Language is our gift and our responsibility. I've come to think of writing as an act of reciprocity with the living land. Words to remember old stories, words to tell new ones, stories that bring science and spirit back together to nurture our becoming people made of corn.